T0132420

Thelma,
The Silly Goose

JUDY HUSTON

Illustration by: Kate Belfy

To order additional copies of this book, contact:
Xlibris
1-888-795-4274
www.Xlibris.com
Orders@Xlibris.com

ISBN: Softcover   978-1-5992-6755-5
        Hardcover   978-1-5992-6756-2

Print information available on the last page

Rev. date: 02/19/2020

GRANDCHILDREN AND COURAGE

TO ALL OF GOD'S CHILDREN, INCLUDING MY GRANDCHILDREN JESSICA, ELIZABETH, TAYLOR AND CAMERON, WHOSE LOVE OF READING AND LOVE OF LIFE, HAS GIVEN ME THE COURAGE TO WRITE THIS BOOK.

TO ALL WHO READ "THELMA'S STORY", I HOPE YOU GET AS MUCH ENJOYMENT FROM READING IT, AS IV'E GOTTEN FROM WRITING IT. AS THELMA WOULD SAY, "LIFE IS GOOD WHEN YOU'RE ALIVE AND BEAUTIFUL"!.

Acknowledgements

My thanks to my husband, Joe, who holds my hand in matters of life and laughter, who provided me with the inspiration for Thelma.

To Kate Belfy, a truly remarkable illustrator who literally brought Thelma to life, and last but not least, Thelma, for just being a "Silly Goose".

Dedication

Hi, my name is Thelma, I'm a Canadian Goose. My story is dedicated to the man, without whose love and nourishing, I would not be here today, Joe Huston. Thanks "Dad", for rescuing me and taking me under "your wing".

Thelma

My story begins when my "Mother Goose" had six baby eggs, then along came Mr. Raccoon and ate all but one, me.

I was left all alone in a nest in the middle of a big swamp and was quickly rescued by a fisherman who saw me from a nearby stream.

He carefully picked me up and gently placed me in the middle of some grass in the front seat of his jeep, for a short, but bumpy ride to my "new home". By the time we arrived, I was almost out of my shell.

Baby goslings (that's what they call baby geese) have a tooth called a pippin tooth, which really comes in handy when you're inside a shell trying to get out and boy, did I want to get out of that eggshell.

You talk about an ugly goose! I was about three inches tall and wet all over, really yucky looking.

After my "Dad" took a big warm towel and dried me off, I became this cute little fluffy yellow bird. Who knew?

My "Dad" then took a big cardboard box and filled it with all kinds of neat things, like twigs, grass, bread and water. This was my new home and I couldn't wait to try it out.

My new home was nice and warm, I had plenty to eat and drink and best of all, I was finally away from Mr. Raccoon. Who could ask for anything more.

After about three months I was getting really big and finally starting to get my feathers, which is a pretty big thing to us birds.

I loved looking at myself in the mirror to see how beautiful I was becoming.

It wasn't long before I was out-growing my "new home" and no matter how I slept, I just couldn't get comfortable.

By this time I was getting pretty lonely, and while my "Dad" was fun to be around, I wished there was another bird to "fly around" with me.

One day, my "Dad" got some kids in the neighborhood to help him. Together, they made me my very own pond. He made benches so people could sit and watch me, brought in more nests and made boxes for the Wood ducks. What a "Dad"!

After awhile, he even brought in more ducks and geese, so I wouldn't be lonely anymore.

After about six months, it was time for me to learn how to fly. I was really scared at first, but after watching the other birds, I said to myself, "Thelma, you can do this, you go girl".

Birds don't come with training wheels like bicycles do, so it took me a while to get my "sea legs".

Now, I weighed about eleven pounds and I was getting pretty good at this "flying business".

My only problem with flying was that I knocked over everything that got in my way. Boy, how I wished I had cruise control!

One Sunday when cars started filling the parking lot at my "Dad's" Church, I decided to see what was going on, so I walked from my Pond in between all the cars to get a better look. Before long, all the other birds were following me. What can I say, I guess I'm just a born leader.

We could never figure out why we couldn't go inside that Church, after all, birds are God's children too!

One of my favorite things to do was watch my "Dad" and his friends play pool. What was the big deal anyway? All you do is push a little ball down a little hole, any bird can do that, nothing to it.

I couldn't wait for my "Dad" to wash his car, I liked grabbing the nozzle of the hose and spraying both of us.

You talk about a "bad feather day"!

Then there was this beagle dog. I never did figure out what his problem was. For some reason, he liked to chase me around water puddles.

I'd wait until he came running over to where I was and then I'd just fly over to the other side. Boy, you talk about a "dumb puppy"!

There was a little old lady that lived across the street, for some reason she just didn't like me. What was there not to like? I was adorable.

She had the biggest porch in the neighborhood so naturally that's where I liked to sleep. She also had the best railings to "pick at" so naturally I did. Why she kept chasing me with that broom, I'll never know.

The one thing I was really good at was flying next to my "Dad's" car. I followed him everywhere. When we came to a stop sign or stop light, I'd just fly over to the other side of the street and wait for him. I might have looked dumb, but I wasn't stupid.

Sometimes, he'd get out of his car and make me fly home. I guess you could say that I was "grounded".

One day my "Dad" decided that I needed a boyfriend. So he started bringing all these Ganders (boy geese) around hoping I'd fall in love with one of them.

But, us girls like to do our own "shopping", so I wouldn't have anything to do with them.

Finally one day, this big handsome gander flew into my pond with great fanfare, honking loudly and I knew the minute I laid my eyes on him, that he was the one for me, my own prince charming.

Once we girls make up our mind, we don't waste any time.

We made our own little nest far away from Mr. Raccoon. Within a few months, I was a "Mother Goose" with six little eggs of my own.

All my babies grew up to be beautiful, just like me. Boy, did I have a story to tell them, about their Mother, a silly goose named Thelma.

The story of Thelma and of her special relationship with Joe Huston is a true story. Thelma, was an "orphan," abandoned in a nest in a swamp which had been destroyed by raccoons, when Joe found her. As Joe's affection for Thelma grew, so did his life long Commitment to the environment and it's habitats. The Hustons were thankful that Thelma came into their lives and in turn enriched not only their family, but their entire neighborhood as well. As for Thelma, she is a 20 year old "Mother Goose" to six beautiful geese all of whom reside in a Bird Sanctuary in Charlotte, Michigan, where the Hustons are frequent visitors. Because Canadian geese have a life Expectancy of 50 years, we expect Thelma To live a long, pampered life. As Thelma would say, "life is good when you are alive and beautiful!"

Thelma And Family

Printed in the United States
By Bookmasters